To the Sea

To the Sea

Thirty Two Poems

From Godey's Lady's Book

Deborah L. Halliday (Editor)

To the Sea
Thirty Two Poems
From Godey's Lady's Book

ISBN: 1500676381
ISBN 13: 9781500676384

First Kindle Edition September 2013
Revised and Expanded Kindle Edition November 2013
First Paperback Edition August 2014

Look On The Sea!

Look on the sea! 'Neath the grand sun, its breast
Glows warm and bright;
But in its depths, where pale the cold pearls rest,
Is darkest night.

~ from "Look on the Sea!" by Emanuel Geibel
Translated by George W. Birdseye.

Table of Contents

INTRODUCTION
The Lady's Book xi
Lady's Book Poetry xii
This Volume xiii

POEMS

To the Sea
by Lydia H. Sigourney 1

Going to Sea
(Author unknown. A children's poem, possibly written by Sarah J. Hale.) 3

Sunrise
by G. W. L. 5

To the Sea
by Rebecca (Portsmouth, N.H.) 7

The Sailor's Adieu to His Wife
by "Lelia Mortimer"
[Dolly Ellen Ring Shepard] 9

Outward Bound
by D. 11

The Seaman's Bride
by "Everallin"
[Marian Means Dix Sullivan] 12

At Sea
by Fritz 14

The Sea Bird
by Bernard Hilton 16

To My Wife
by Isaac Moise 19

I Love the Sea, the Mighty Sea
by J. Q. P. (Elizabeth City, N. C.) 21

Calm at Sea
by William Gilmore Simms 23

Like Music Stealing O'er the Water
by [L. McCartney Montagu.] 25

The Stormy Petrel
by "Barry Cornwall"
[Bryan Waller Procter] 27

Song to the Sea-Wave
by R. James Keeling 29

The Storm at Sea
by Mrs. Elizabeth D. Harrington 31

Apostrophe to the Sea
by William Gilmore Simms 33

The Light-House Keeper's Daughter
by Theo. D. C. Miller, M.D. 36

Gone Down at Sea
by George R. Calvert 38

Hope
by Anna Maria Wells 40

The Waves and Their Dead
by "Maurice O'Quill, Esq."
[Martin Van Buren Dinslow] 44

Little Maud
by Lucia S. Alden 48

The Deep
by John Gardiner Calkins Brainard 50

The Dead at Sea
by Thomas Dunn English 52

Sonnet: The Sea
by William Alexander 54

The Dying Sailor To His Shipmates
by James T. Fields 55

To A Sea Gull
by Isaac McLellan, Jr. 57

Sonnet: Ocean
by William Alexander 61

Ocean Music at Evening
by Mary E. Lee 62

"The Fairy of the Foam"
by A. Cleveland Cox, Esq. 63

The Sea
by [Thomas Campbell] 65

By the Summer Sea
by A. M. Dana 66

SOURCES 69

Introduction
The Lady's Book

Godey's *Lady's Book* was one of the most popular American magazines of the nineteenth century. Founded in 1830 and hitting its circulation peak in the 1850s, the *Lady's Book's* subscription list crossed the nation, the continent, and indeed the globe.

The *Lady's Book* was established in Philadelphia by Louis A. Godey. It was an enterprising move on his part, a bold venture into the sea of new magazines aimed at women. The country was young and expanding rapidly, and advances in transportation and printing had opened the doors for mass production and distribution of periodi cal literature. Godey entered a crowded field where early competitors had experienced neither success nor longevity. Initially Godey followed the common practice of simply copying material from British and other American publications (for free and often without attribution; lack of copyright protection made this commonplace and expected) adding some new material, and relying on packaging and marketing to differentiate his product. Somehow it worked.

His confidence, personality, and business ability served him well, and by mid-decade he had the capital to expand. He began his search for an editor, someone who could help him to grow his *Lady's Book* into the premier magazine in the nation for women. There was one person who had all the right qualifications, a woman editor running her own magazine in Boston: Sarah Josepha Hale.

Hale's *American Ladies' Magazine* was in its ninth year of publication. When she began the magazine in 1828 she announced a policy that was at the time both risky and revolutionary: she would publish only original articles, not re-prints or pirated material. She also began, after the initial issues, to pay authors for their work. She encouraged American authorship on American themes, and supported efforts of new authors as well as those more established and well-known. She focused on quality, and made it her mission to bring an intellectually and morally elevated level of literature to her readers. Unfortunately her expenses made her financially vulnerable to economic downturns, and in the downturn of the mid-1830's her publication was struggling financially. Godey's offer came at the right time; in 1836 the two publications merged, and *Godey's Lady's Book and the American Ladies' Magazine* went on to make publication history.

Lady's Book Poetry

Poetry was an important component of the magazine for both Godey and Hale; it was important to readers as well. Nineteenth century Americans commonly read poetry, wrote poetry, and expected to find poetry utilized as an elevated and creative way to express both feelings and ideas. The poetry found in *Godey's* was often reader-submitted; among the thousands of poems published over the decades, in addition to poems by well-known authors such as Lydia Sigourney, George P. Morris, Elizabeth Ellet, Hannah F. Gould, Frances Osgood, William Gilmore Simms and Elizabeth Oakes Smith, there are myriads of poems by unknown or amateur authors, many of whom used pseudonyms so that we don't know their identities even today.

The authors of the poems in this volume might be familiar or unfamiliar; they might have published extensively or this might have been the only poem they ever published. What is important to know is that their poetry was an authentic expression of their experience and their times; as such, it can both speak to us through our common emotions and teach us about a time we cannot experience directly.

This Volume

The nineteenth century was still the age of sail; ships not only crossed the globe but also served much of the country's population by transporting a wide variety of commercial goods and passengers. Railroads had begun moving both people and goods between centers of commerce as early as the 1830s, but a coastal journey by ship was fast and efficient as long as nothing went wrong. Port cities (large and small) up and down the east coast carried on lively domestic and foreign trade, and much of the nation's population lived near the coasts. It was natural to express one's relationship with the ocean in poetry; the sea was, and still is, a powerful and awe inspiring force of nature.

Modern weather forecasting was in its infancy in the nineteenth century and depended on communication of local weather conditions from one part of the country to another. Those communication capabilities did not help sailors already at sea; they were at the mercy of the elements with little hope of rescue in the event of a shipwreck. Death at sea was a real possibility, and in some areas coastal residents sometimes found bodies of unknown men and women washed up on shore. Saying goodbye to a loved one at the start of a voyage came with the recognition that the voyager might not return. Many sailors and travelers counted on prayer to save them from the perils of the ocean, but maintained faith that God would care for them if death came. *Godey's* published numerous poems about shipwrecks (most not included here), probably because the connection to the experience was so real for readers.

"The Lighthouse Keeper's Daughter" is a tribute to an actual person – Ida Lewis, of Newport, Rhode Island – who unofficially took over the duties of lighthouse keeper from her father after he suffered a stroke. She continued to maintain the light for many years, saving ships from ruin in this busy and rocky seaport area. Lewis became nationally famous in her unconventional role and was considered a heroine for her ability and dedication. The poem was written by Theodore D. C. Miller, M.D., who also wrote lyrics for several published hymns.

Several of the poets in this volume were professional and prolific writers whose names are still recognized today in connection with nineteenth century

American literature. James T. Fields, Lydia Sigourney, William Gilmore Simms, Anna Maria Wells, and George W. Birdseye were all well-known American poets who published frequently in *Godey's*. Hale's publishing relationship with both Sigourney and Wells had begun as early as 1828 in the *Ladies' Magazine*; six of the poems in this collection, including those by Sigourney and Wells, were taken from the *Ladies' Magazine* prior to its merger with *Godey's*. Other poets in this collection were less well known, but did publish beyond *Godey's*. Lucia S. Alden, distant cousin to H. W. Longfellow, occasionally published both prose and poetry in literary periodicals, and Mary E. Lee was a published poet. William Alexander had at least 100 sonnets published in *Godey's* between 1849 and 1860, but it is not clear whether this particular William Alexander published elsewhere. "Lelia Mortimer" was the pseudonym of Dolly Ellen Ring Shepard (Mrs. D. Ellen Goodman Shepard) who published in the periodical literature of the day (*Cut-flowers: A Collection of Poems*, 1854). "Maurice O'Quill, Esq." was the pseudonym used by Martin Van Buren Denslow (*Good Literature*, 1882).

In some cases the names printed in *Godey's* might represent typographical errors; in the era before typewriters, when printers by necessity worked from handwritten manuscripts, errors could easily be introduced. With that in mind, A. Cleveland Cox, Esq. is likely Arthur Cleveland Coxe, published poet and later bishop in the Episcopal church; George R. Calvert is possibly poet George H. Calvert. Isaac McLellan's name was printed as "J. McLellan" above his poem "To a Sea Gull;" his identity as the author is confirmed through later publication of a variant of the poem.

Thomas Campbell and Barry Cornwall (actually Bryan Waller Procter) were well-known British poets in the nineteenth century. Campbell's poem appeared in *Godey's* as an unattributed extract from his longer poem "Lines on the View from St. Leonard's." Cornwall's poem "The Stormy Petrel" was published in his book *English Songs, and Other Small Poems* and appeared in *Godey's* as a song set to music by W. D. Brinklé, M.D., a frequent music contributor.

Some of the poems in this volume are brutal depictions of nature and the raw power of the sea while others emphasize its beauty and calming effect. Many reflect the impact the sea can have on human lives, and the sadness of never really knowing the fate of a loved one last seen departing aboard a ship. Although the circumstances of our lives have changed since the nineteenth century, the vastness of the ocean has not; we still stand humbled by it.

To The Sea

by Lydia Huntley Sigourney

Grant me thy company, thou solemn sea!
Earth speaks of man—her trimly trellised walks,
Her groves, her gardens, and her gorgeous domes,
All speak of man. Even the pure, lofty sky,
With all its change of garniture—its robe
Of morning purple, and its garb by day
Of blue and silver tissue, richly wrought,
Its mantle for the eve, of nameless dyes—
Oft seems to me (may Heaven forgive the thought!)
Like some fair woman in her coquetry.
        But *thou dost speak of God*, thou holy Sea!
Thou wonder-working, mortal-mocking One.
Alone upon thy shore I rove, and count
The crested billows in their ceaseless play;
And when dense darkness shrouds thy awful face,

I listen to thy voice, and bow me down
In all my nothingness to *Him* whose eye
Beholds thy congregated world of waves
But as a noteless dew-drop.

Going To Sea

(Author unknown. A children's poem, possibly written by Sarah J. Hale.)

Hark!—hear ye the signal?
The breezes are steady,
The anchor is weighing,
And we must be ready:
Farewell, my dear mother,
I fear thou'lt be lonely,
But oh! do not sorrow—
I'll think of thee only.

And dread not the danger,
Though I'm on the billow:
I know my kind Saviour
Will watch o'er my pillow;
The sea own'd his sceptre
When its path he was treading,
The wind and the waters
Grew calm at his bidding.

We'll trust him, we'll trust him,
We'll pray and he'll hear us;
On land or on water
Alike he'll be near us:
Let this song bear to him
Our heart's fond devotion—
And under his guidance
I'll launch on the ocean.

Sunrise

BY *G. W. L.*

Night's curtain parted in the east—
And the strong brave sun came up;
And with his banner streaming wide,
Gleamed on the mountain top.

Between the sun and hanging clouds
A light green sea was spread;
And a trembling star looked out on it
Like an angel's eye in dread.

The brilliant sunbeams thickly fell—
And the sea was changed to gold;
And sparkling streams, in yellow curls,
Leaped onward bright and bold.

The moon still lingered on the blue,
But a dying light she gave—
Now fading quite—now beaming faint—
She sunk to her blue grave.

Then upward!—up! In silent march
Went the proud and noble sun—
And the green earth smiled, and the ocean gleamed,
Till his flaming course was done.

To The Sea

by Rebecca (Portsmouth, N.H.)

The sea—the sea—the silent sea,
So faithless, yet so fair;
O, who to-night could gaze on thee,
And dream of evil there?

The sea—the sea—the silent sea,
So eloquent of rest;
Yet millions who have trusted thee,
Have perished on thy breast.

Amid the elemental strife
Their wail has pierced the sky,
As clinging fearfully to life,
They sought thy depths—to die!

Dread element unfathomed, dark,
Inscrutable to man,
Who may those waves descend and mark?
Those deep recesses scan?

O, who shall dare those depths untried,
Where centuries have slept,
And navies perished in their pride,
Unwitnessed and unwept?

Who, who, his victor brow may grace
With ocean's sunless wreath,
As fearlessly he stoops to trace
Thy triumph march, O death?

The sea—the sea—the silent sea,
God's minister of might!
I marvel, as I gaze on thee,
Beneath the pale moonlight.

The Sailor's Adieu to His Wife

BY "LELIA MORTIMER"
[DOLLY ELLEN RING SHEPARD]

One moment longer I may gaze on thee—
One little moment lingering may stay,
Ere o'er the billows of yon trackless sea
In my proud, noble ship I take my way.
One moment, and I leave thee for long years—
Leave thee alone, in sorrow and tears.

My own, my precious wife, look up once more
With the deep, melting sunlight of thine eyes;
Their glance shall be the ray to guide me o'er
The treacherous waves 'neath the dark, gloomy skies;
Let but one smile about thy lips play,
And it shall cheer me on my lonely way.

No—no: Thou art clinging wildly to my neck;
I feel thy scalding tears upon my cheek;
My own are falling and I cannot check

Their course—and yet, with faltering tongue I speak
This sad farewell, and from thy drooping brow
Turn me away amid thy sobbings low.

Hush, dear one; to the care of Him who sees
From his bright throne above our griefs and tears,
I leave thee. I shall hear upon the breeze
His voice, and its low tone shall quell my fears,
Telling that thou, in this dear home, are blest—
And bringing to my heart a happy rest.

Then look once more, with thy holy eyes,
Into my own; and let me know that thou
Wilt nightly kneel, and to the calm, deep skies,
With humble heart, lifting this youthful brow,
Wilt pray for him who far upon the sea,
Will dream and think alone of heaven and thee.

And now farewell—one kiss upon thy cheek;
One pressure of thy white and trembling hand—
And once more, dearest, of thy deep love speak,
And I go forth to join the faithful band
Who wait their leader; then, upon the sea,
I wander for long years, and dream of thee.

Outward Bound

BY *D.*

Solemn and beautiful, the night hours on the sea!
The sun hath sunk to rest in silent majesty.
In the pure blue above, mark now each radiant star—
Diamonds in night's dark robe—glistening afar.
My mother gazes there, and thinks of me away,
Whose floating home they cheer: Then mother, dearest, pray—
Pray Heaven to guide thy wanderer safely o'er the deep—
Pray Heaven to guard us all, while we in quiet sleep!

Solemn and beautiful, the night hours on the sea!
Slowly the moon ascends in silent majesty.
Mark how each silver wave smiles 'neath her gentle beam,
Laving our bark's smooth side with fitful gleam;
Wide spread the waters round—in seeming mirth they play,
Sporting on unseen graves: Then mother dearest, pray—
Pray Heaven to guide thy wanderer safely o'er the deep—
Pray Heaven to guard us all, while we in quiet sleep.

The Seaman's Bride

BY "EVERALLIN"
[MARIAN MEANS DIX SULLIVAN]

Thour't far away, my own love,
Beyond our rainbow's sweep—
And beating on the waters
Of the mighty southern deep.

The gale that thins our forest
Shall bring no change to thee—
The wind that fills thy sails
May not breathe of love to me.

Were't not for this fair sleeping girl,
And him, thy bright-haired boy,
I'd rove with thee the ocean wide,
Companion of thy joy.

We've skimmed the billows cheerily,
Nor cared for all beside,

Thou the youthful master then,
And I the rosy bride.

I've stood upon the deck with thee,
When waves were dashing high,
And flung my tresses joyously
To the wild winds raging by.

And now with these our loved ones,
I pass the cheerful day,
But sadly fall the evening shades,
For thou art far away.

Oh, fling out all thy white sails,
And hither, hither come—
And heaven speed the southern breeze,
To waft thee to thy home.

At Sea

BY FRITZ

A summer eve, and the summer sea
Lies down to its quiet sleep;
And the beams are dancing merrily
Of stars on the slumbering deep;
And the Queen of Night
Casts her pallid light
On the vista of waters blue,
While each tapering spar
Throws the picture far
Of the moon from its canvas new.

Our good bark speeds, for she's homeward bound—
Speeds on o'er the trackless sea;
Ay bright the waters are glancing round
The bow of the "Arabie;"
And the zephyrs sigh
In the star-gemmed sky,
And the trades blow cheerily behind;

And the rattling shroud
Pipes a chorus loud
To the singing harp of the wind.

Sweet music rings on the sluggish wings
Of the dull and dreamy air,
And loud it sings as it strangely brings
To the watcher, pictures rare—
Of the dead men cast
In the charnel vast
Of their grave, the yawning deep,
Down under the surge—
And the solemn dirge
It sounds, o'er the sailors' sleep.

At sea, at sea, to the brave and free
There's "life on the ocean wave,"
And noble joy's in the sailor's glee
As he sails – sails over his grave!
Not where winds blow shrill
On the village hill,
Nor down in the flowery lea—
But afar o'er the deep
There's a quiet sleep;
And the dead rest well in the sea.

The Sea Bird

BY ***BERNARD HILTON***

Bird of the deep,
That still around keep'st thy mournful way,
Thou hast a purpose in the dreary play
Which thou dost keep.

Why wouldst thou roam,
We ask—misdeeming of thy natural powers,
Thy wants, still shaped in fancy such as ours,
Which long for home—

Here, where no shore,
No jutting rock, invites thy drooping wing,
When thou art weary, on its cliffs to cling,
Thy journey o'er?

What food the sea
Bestows, what refuge when the storm is nigh,

What joy the zephyr soft, the clear blue sky,
Are dark to me!

But in our pride,
It may rejoice us to assume thee sent
To glad the gloom of our imprisonment,
Our course to guide;

Perchance to bring,
To cheer the mariner doubtful of his way,
Tidings of rocky shore and fertile bay,
And sweet, cool spring.

Thy laws, like ours,
Make grateful the due service, wild or strange;
And whether in adventure still we range,
Or keep close bowers,

The pleasure still
Compensates for the perils and the pains
If each, obeying what the sire ordains,
Sinks his own will.

The sea is thine;
Thy nest of foam receives thee as the day
Closes, and morning still, upon thy way
On the deep brine.

Wild is thy note,
And, to our senses, ominous; but thy young

Hearken, and answer with each happy tongue
And screaming throat.

They find their rest
Where we lose ours—the wild, blue heaving wave
Rocks them—and where our forms would find a grave,
They find a nest!

Thou teachest right;
Day over, with its triumphs and its storms,
How small the care where we should cast our forms
For sleep at night.

To My Wife

BY ISAAC MOISE

Written while on my passage to France

The moon is rising from the sea,
The waves are dashing on our lee,
The dew is falling from above—
Farewell to thee, my wife! My love!

The moon is silvering with its light
The ocean foam—so pure, so bright;
The stars are sparkling from above—
Farewell, my wife! My only love!

The moon is rising now on high—
I gaze upon her, and I sigh;
Her mellow light shines from above,
On all on earth I fondly love.

The moon is waning while I write—
An envious cloud obscures her light;
No longer shines she from above—
Farewell, my wife! My only love!

The moon has sunk beneath the wave;
Like those we love sink to the grave;
Now darkness dwells around, above—
Farewell! Farewell! My only love!

I Love the Sea, the Mighty Sea

BY J. Q. P. (ELIZABETH CITY, N.C.)

Oh I love the sea, the mighty sea,
When the big waves lash the sky;
If my ship is strong as we bound along,
There's none so merry as I.
Then give me the sea, the boundless sea,
Where May ever roam,
Afar from the strife of a stifled life,
I ask no better home.

When the sky is dark, and my gallant bark
Is bounding o'er the sea,
Let the lightning flash, and the billows dash;
They cannot frighten me.
Let the thunders roll, and from pole to pole,
Wake air, and sea, and shore;
Secure I sleep, for God will keep
Me safe midst the tempest's roar.

But a frightful sight is the blacksome night,
When far away from land,
The shivering sail in the passing gale
Is torn by an unseen hand;
And all around is an ominous sound
That soon the sea may be,
Dashing its waves o'er our floating graves
And we in eternity.

Yet I love to sweep o'er the "vasty deep"
When the waves run mountain high,
To hear the mast in a fearful blast
As the winds howl sadly by;
For then I feel, as in prayer I kneel,
That He who reigns on high
Is able to save from a watery grave
And will hear our dying cry.

Oh I love the sea, the mighty sea,
When the big waves lash the sky,
If my ship is strong as we bound along,
There's none so merry as I.
Then give me the sea, the boundless sea,
Where I may ever roam,
Afar from the strife of a stifled life,
And I ask no better home.

Calm at Sea

BY WILLIAM GILMORE SIMMS

Calm on the deep! The heavy sail
Hangs lifeless from the mast;
The sea, without a single gale,
Appears to sleep at last;
And peering in its face, the sun
Looks down with burning light,
Till far as eye can stretch, his one
Rich mirror hangs in sight.

A world from all the world apart,
Chained idly on the sea,
How droops the eye, how sinks the heart,
Vain, wishing to be free!
How dread the fear that fills the thought,
That winds may never rise—
Thirsting, yet fastened to the spot
Beneath those burning skies.

The pirate rears his bloody flag,
And leaves the Cuba shore;
Blow, breezes, blow, for if ye lag
We hail our homes no more;
And should our hapless fate be such
We'll wrong not nature so,
To think that hearts who've sighed so much
Will soon forget their woe.

Ripple, ye waters, into smiles,
The sun's vast mirror break,
Whilst far Bahama's dreary isles
Shall vanish in our wake.
Nor should your storms affright us more—
Blow, tempests of the deep;
I better love old ocean's roar
Than this, his stagnant sleep.

Like Music Stealing O'er the Water

[L. McCartney Montagu]

Like music stealing o'er the water
At even tide when winds are still,
Sweet thoughts of him around me gather
And all my heart with music fill;
And as I watch the moon above me
With all her bright and starry train,
I pray for him who vowed to love me,
Now sailing on the distant main.

At midnight, when the storm is raging,
It sounds to me my sailor's knell;
I see him with the wild waves striving,
I hear him sigh his last farewell;
Oh! would I were like those above me!
A spirit freed from mortal chain,
To watch o'er him who vowed to love me,
When sailing on the distant main.

Oh mother dear, forbear to reason!
Oh sister dear, forbear to chide!
As landsmen's wives, ye cannot measure
The sorrows of a sailor's bride.
Your partings are too short to move ye;
But years may pass, if e'er again,
I look on him who vowed to love me,
Returning from the distant main.

The Stormy Petrel

BY "BARRY CORNWALL"
[BRYAN WALLER PROCTER]

A thousand miles from land we are,
Tossing about on the roaring sea,
From billow to bounding billow cast
Like fleecy snow on the stormy blast;
The sails are scattered abroad like weeds—
The strong masts shake like quivering reeds—
The mighty cables and iron chains—
The hull which all earthly strength disdains—
They strain and they crack, and hearts like stone,
Their natural, hard proud strength disown.

Up and down! Up and down!
From the base of the wave to the billow's crown;
And amidst the flashing and feathery foam,
The Stormy Petrel finds a home—
A home, if such a place may be
For her who lives on the wide, wide sea,

On the craggy ice, in the frozen air,
And only seeketh her rocky lair
To warm her young and teach them to spring
At once o'er the waves on their stormy wing!

O'er the deep! O'er the deep!
Where the whale, and the shark, and the sword-fish sleep,
Outflying the blast and the driving rain,
The Petrel telleth her tale in vain—
For the mariner curseth the warning bird,
Who bringeth him news of the storm unheard!
Ah, thus does the prophet of good or ill
Meet hate from the creatures he serveth still;
Yet he ne'er falters. So Petrel! Spring
Once more o'er the waves on thy stormy wing!

Song to the Sea-Wave

BY R. JAMES KEELING

Wave of the ocean waste! Canst speak to me?
The winds are sinking to their caverned rest,
The day's last beam hath faded o'er the sea,
And glorious stars are mirrored on its breast!
Wave of the deep blue sea, let's talk awhile.

We know that thou hast heard the fearful moan
Rise upward with the drowning sea-boy's cry;
And e'en while dreaming of his cottage home,
Far, far away beneath a golden sky,
Thy careless voice hath roused him up to die.

We know too thou hast dashed in fearful glee
O'er the proud argosies that crossed thy way;
Hast felt the wind, in revel wild and free,
Sweep round thy form and curl thee into spray—
And yet thou wanderest here, child of the sea.

But tell us of the ocean dead, thou wave—
Say: do they sleep in calm and quiet now?
Do thy wild brothers hold their restless rave
Around each form, and o'er each marble brow?
Or do they sleep the slumber of the grave?

In the dim palaces of ocean's caves,
Where the sea-maiden weaves her coral wreath,
Are there no sighing winds and moonlit waves?
No flashing stars that tremble far beneath,
Lighting the sea-tomb with a quenchless ray?

Methinks thou'rt murmuring now: beneath the seas
There is a scene more beautiful than ours,
Whose gorgeous palaces and coral trees,
Imbedded mid rich gems and pearly flowers,
Smile like the visioned Paradise of God.

And there, amid that strange and gorgeous home,
Roam the freed spirits of the ocean dead;
Far from the strife of earth, alone, alone,
With a green canopy o'erhead,
Mid the wild music of the sea they dwell.

Stray child of ocean, art thou weary now?
Cease thy wild moan—thy life will soon be o'er;
A shroud of foam has gathered on thy brow—
There, thou art breaking on the silent shore—
Wave of the deep blue sea, thou art no more!

The Storm at Sea

BY MRS. ELIZABETH D. HARRINGTON

Hark! in the deep breathed thunder of the waves!
Hark! how rich with demon voice and demon might,
They sound through all their dark and solemn caves—
War's dreadful alarm to the ear of night!

Fierce to the battle, lo! how swift they fly!
Swelling and foaming in their mad career!
Their silver banners now salute the sky—
Now sinking, mingle with the darkness drear!

Fiercer and fiercer wears the frantic night!
Million on million voices stun the air!
The mighty winds come howling to the fight,
Like long-pent lions bounding from their lair!

Its brilliant horror now the lightning lends!
The pealing thunder mingles with the roar
Of falling torrents, and wild Tumult rends
Sea, air, and heaven, from shore to viewless shore!

Unearthly sounds! Sweet Sleep, affrighted, sighs,
Spreads her soft wings, and flies your harsh domain;
While Terror pale, with strained and fiery eyes,
And silent Awe begin their solemn reign!

God—in the hollow of thy hand we lie!
Death's eager shaft is round us and above;
But clear-eyed Faith, all trustful, points on high
To that blest beacon-light, thy perfect love.

Apostrophe to the Sea

BY WILLIAM GILMORE SIMMS

WRITTEN ON MY FIRST VOYAGE

I hear thee through thy voices, mighty sea!
I watch thee through thy billows, never stayed.
Thine is the sleepless march of destiny;
Thine is the might, in majesty arrayed,
That mocks the ambitious, makes the fond afraid,
Laughing alike at human strength and prayer,
Rolling thy sullen waves o'er hearts that made
Their trust in thee to waft them to the dear,
Who still survey thy deeps in hopefulness and fear!

The awe that is unbounded fills my soul
As I behold thee, limitless and lone,
Driving still onward, scorning all control;
Keeping thy march that never may be done
While man surveys thee, and the revered sun

Directs thy course along the mighty deeps.
Thou seekest a goal that never may be won,
With race for aye renewing. Seldom sleeps
Thy wing that never tires, thy form that never creeps.

The frail barque bears me, bounding o'er thy breast;
Yet am I not thy master! In my hand
I grasp no bridle which shall bid thee rest,
No curb which may subdue thee to command,
No scourge to make thee tremble and to stand;
Thou laugh'st at human conqueror—though thy mood,
The mood of power in sport, at moments bland,
Moves thee to yield a pathway through thy flood
To him who seeks for sway through darker seas of blood.

* * *

The winds that gather on thy breast by night,
Bear to the distant cities all the tale
Thou deign'st them, of the forms which in their sight
Held hearts most precious! Thou hast heard the wail
That followed thy dread tidings, and thy gale
Has mocked their griefs and now aroused their fears
For others like the lost ones, who make sail
Trusting thy mercies! Many a watcher hears
Thy storms that rise by night, with trembling and in tears.

The thin plank only keeps me from thy grasp;
The thin sail only lifts me o'er thy breast;
Thy mighty arms seem stretching out to clasp—
Thy mighty passions, in thy roar expressed,

Seem toiling now, and bounding to arrest
The flight of thy new victim! Madly glare
Thy vengeful eyes of terror! Thou would'st wrest
Thy prey, despite the mercy which would spare—
The mercy born of love, sole sovereign everywhere!

* * *

That love shall spell thy tempests, mighty sea!
Its voice of power is on thee, and confessed,
Thy tossing limbs are fettered! Thou shalt be
Subdued, even as an infant sunk to rest—
Thou, that with giant limbs and heaving breast
Strove against the heavens, and leagued with storm, arose
Like one with fiendish enemies possessed,
Mad with unmeasured wrath, still prompt for blows,
Denied repose thyself, denying all repose!

Roll on! Roll on! Thy billows bear me far—
And if my bones must whiten in the wave
Beneath the influence of malignant star,
I would not ask from fate a kinder grave,
Nor offer up the homage which might save!
It might be longer life were longer woe;
And he whom fortune still hath willed to brave,
Might, safely rendered to his home below,
Find young affection's tear had long since ceased to flow.

The Light-House Keeper's Daughter

BY THEO. D. C. MILLER, M.D.

The light-house keeper was old and weak,
And the night was dark and drear;
The winter breezes were chill and bleak,
And a fearful storm was near.
The lights were out, and no help at hand,
And the poor old man could see
The sails so white, as they neared the land,
From over the foam-capped sea.

There were hidden rocks off wrecker's cave,
And the dark-browed men were there,
Who gazed with joy on each storm-lashed wave
And the ships they hoped to snare.
The winds grew fierce, and their false lights shone
Far over the angry sea;
The weird shapes crept o'er their eyrie lone,
While they drank and danced in glee.

The old keeper's eyes were dim with tears
As the false lights shone afar;
Each flash of lightening woke his fears,
For nearer came sails and spar.
With a sigh he turned from the cruel sight,
And his heart with grief was sore;
For wrecks and sorrow would come that night,
And dear ones would meet no more.

A step, and the old door opens wide,
And a maiden, sweet and fair,
The keeper's daughter, is by his side,
Then on like a flash up stair.
With eyes of fire, and a firm, strong hand,
She runs up the lanterns three:
Then falls in a faint–while on to land
The ships come safe o'er the sea.

Gone Down at Sea

BY GEORGE R. CALVERT

A deep, black scowl spreads o'er the sky,
No angel eyes smile down,
While ocean's raging, foaming wave
Leaps toward the storm-god's throne.
Oh, 'tis a fear-inspiring sight,
The shade of seaman's doom,
When a rayless, warring, tempest night
Pipes to his last, long home!

All wildly leaps the gallant ship,
And men inured to care,
With sinking heart and trembling lip
Are yielding to despair.
The pumps! The pumps! A leak! A leak!
Rings out full loud and clear,
While thought usurps the power to speak
From those who battle there.

Yet many an eye is doomed to keep
Watch o'er the sea in vain;
And many a widow dreams in sleep
The ship's come back again,
But wakes to live in hopes and fears
Until the truth *must* be
In those sad words—so fraught with tears—
Gone down! Gone down at sea!

The morning breaks with rosy light;
The waves now sink to rest;
But down below, eternal night
Reigns in each silent breast.
'Tis this that makes pale Luna roam,
And heave, for tears, the wave
For those who leave a happy home
To find an ocean grave.

Hope

BY ANNA MARIA WELLS

There sits a woman on the brow
Of yonder rocky height;
There, gazing over the waves below,
She sits from morn till night.

She heeds not how the mad waves leap
Along the rugged shore;
She looks for one upon the deep
She never may see more.

As morning twilight faintly gleams,
Her shadowy form I trace;
Wrapped in the slivery mist she seems
The genius of the place.

Far other once was Rosalie.
Her smile once was glad; her voice
Like music o'er a summer sea,
Said to the heart—rejoice!

O'er her pure thoughts, did sorrow fling
Perchance a shade, 't would pass
Lightly, as glides the breath of Spring
Along the bending grass.

A sailor's bride 'twas hers to be:
Wo to the faithless main!
Nine summers since, he went to sea
And ne'er returned again.

But long—where all is wrecked beside
And every joy is chased—
Long, long will lingering hope abide
Amid the dreary waste.

Nine years. Though all have given him o'er,
Her spirit doth not fail;
And still she waits along the shore
The never coming sail.

On that high rock, abrupt and bare,
She ever sits, as now;
The dews have damped her flowing hair—
The sun has scorched her brow.

And every far-off sail she sees,
And every passing cloud,
Or white-winged sea-bird on the breeze,
She calls to it aloud.

The sea-bird answers to her cry;
The cloud, the sail, float on;
The hoarse wave mocks her misery—
Yet is her hope not gone.

It cannot go—were that to part,
So long, so faintly nursed,
So mingled with her faithful heart,
That heart itself would burst.

When falling dews the clover steep,
And birds are in their nest,
And flower-buds folded up to sleep,
And ploughmen gone to rest,

Down the rude track her feet have worn
Where scarce the goat may go—
Poor Rosalie, with forlorn look,
Is seen descending slow.

But when the gray morn tints the sky
And lights that lofty peak,
With strange luster in her eye,
A fever in her cheek,

Again she goes, untired, to sit
And watch the live-long day;
Nor till the star of eve is lit,
E'er turns her steps away.

Hidden, and deep, and never dry,
Or slowing, or at rest,
A living spring of hope doth lie
In every human breast.

All else may fail that soothes the heart—
All, save that fount alone;
With that and life at once we part:
For life and hope are one.

The Waves and Their Dead

BY "MAURICE O'QUILL, ESQ." [MARTIN VAN BUREN DENSLOW]

A darksome billow shoreward wends its way;
And as 'tis mounting solemn to the strand,
Its crest uncapped of foam's pearl-glittering spray,
It steps the measured tread of funeral band
That silent, bears the bier of some unknown
Whose mystery the concourse tempts alone.

The pregnant, sabled wave rolls up the shore;
It pauses there awhile, and then unfolds
Its laden breast, that sullen, yields its store—
As if it were the fearful pall that holds,
Enwrapt in lingering, jealous, clasped embrace,
The spoils of pain brought near their resting place.

Then summoning its scattered waters back,
It heaves their volume off in hurried course
And blends with other waves as rude and black,

To lose its own identity—and hoarse,
To revel wild—as if its roar would hush
Upbraidings moaned by winds that o'er it rush.

'Twas to confide to tombings of the sand
The victim of its 'gulphing wantonness
The billow stole thus lonely to the strand—
As will assassins seek the wilderness,
To press in earth's unwilling, heaving breast
Dread secrets which in consequence ne'er can rest.

But mark, upon the bleak and boundless shore,
Among the riven timbers of a wreck,
A mangled mass that once man's semblance bore,
And whose hand dreamt it could the tempest check.
A wear'some toy, the waves have cast it there,
As all of him who would their warnings dare!

A playful wave trips onward in its dance,
And heedless—like a merry, thoughtless child,
Whose race amid the swollen graves will chance
To bound from mound to mound in gambol wild—
Strews its glistening, gaily rattling pearls,
And o'er the corpse their sparkling host unfurls.

But see how shudders each retreating gem!
And how the quivering crowd together clings,
As other coursings it would backward stem,
Yet needs must sweep the dead, o'er which it flings
A snow-white shroud—with earth's symbolic mite—
A pious, friendly hand's last solemn rite!

The tremulous and conscious wavelet fled,
And deeply sighed a wailing funeral note
Which o'er the briny waste in sadness sped,
And sought deep caverned harps to set afloat
A louder strain—the stern, majestic dirge
Earth moans above the dark deeds of the surge!

The gentle billow meets a sister wave,
And leads it softly to the mournful spot,
Whose awful gloom with less of fear they brave;
And then embraced, as if both wed in thought,
They pause, and turn afresh upon the sea,
Whilst rippling into tear-drops noiselessly.

They pour the fullness of their sorrow's weight
Upon a stouter wave's expansive breast,
Which heaves responsive sighs that such a fate
Befell creation's proudest work, and best;
Then slowly moving to the charneled strand,
They gather o'er the corpse a mound of sand.

And oft these weeping, sympathetic waves
Will noiseless steal to that sepulchral spot,
And, blending genial swellings, tearful lave
The sandy mound, till underwashings blot
From off the desert strand's outstretching face,
Each vestige of the victim's slumbering place.

And thus from life's tempestuous ocean prest,
Is tossed on death's dark circumambient strand,
Humanity—whose wreck sinks there to rest,
And where approach awhile a wailing band
Who let Time's wave the sad spot wear away,
But blend remembrance with eternity.

Little Maud

BY LUCIA S. ALDEN

Where over the loose gray sands
The waters come and go,
A thousand flashing hands,
Flashing and white as snow,
Beckon, beckon, beckon,
Through gathered gloom and mist–
Flexile, sinuous hands
Beckon through gloom and mist.

All through the storm's uproar,
Softer sounds touch my ear–
Wooing murm'rous laughter,
And voices pure and clear,
Calling, calling, calling,
"Come to us Maud, oh come!"
Wooing, murm'rous voices,
Calling, "Little Maud, come!"

And I am little Maud;
Over the sands I run,
Light as down of thistles
Blown about in the sun.
My hair is fine and straight,
And streams out on the gale,
And as a midnight wraith
My face is wan and pale.

Drenched with the fog I lie
Upon the storm-seared rocks;
Below, the rollers beat
With awful, thunderous shocks.
All through the seething foam
The beckoning hands I see;
All through the storm's uproar
The voices call to me.

And the hands are soft and white,
Flashing and white like snow;
The voices pure and sweet,
Wooing, and soft, and low.
'Tis I, little Maud, they call,
And one day I will go
There where white hands beckon,
And voices woo me so.

The Deep

BY JOHN GARDINER CALKINS BRAINARD

There's beauty in the deep.
The wave is bluer than the sky,
And though the light shines bright on high,
More softly do the sea gems glow
That sparkle in the depths below;
The rainbow's tints are only made
When on the waters they are laid,
And Sun and Moon most sweetly shine
Upon the ocean's level brine;
There's beauty in the deep.

There's music in the deep;
It is not in the surf's rough roar,
Nor in the whispering, shelly shore—
They are but earthly sounds, that tell
How little of the sea-nymph's shell
That sends its loud, clear note abroad,
Or winds its softness through the flood,

Echoes through groves with coral gay
And dies, on spongy hanks, away.
There's music in the deep.

There's quiet in the deep.
Above, let tides and tempests rave,
And earth-born whirlwinds wake the wave;
Above, let care and fear contend
With sin and sorrow to the end:
Here, far beneath the tainted foam
That frets above our peaceful home,
We dream in joy, and wake in love,
Nor know the rage that yells above.
There's quiet in the deep.

The Dead At Sea

BY *THOMAS DUNN ENGLISH*

In the far, deep sea,
There lies he.
Over his bare bones the sea-weed twines,
And branch and blossom water-vines.
Around, to ornament his head,
Are trees of coral, white and red;
And the fish as they glide, to and fro,
Look with surprise
From their glassy eyes,
On the whitening bones of Joe—poor Joe!
The whitening bones of Joe.

In the far, deep sea,
There is he.
Never again shall he tread the land,
And warmly press his comrade's hand,
Nor rain, nor sunshine, calm nor storm
Shall fill with life his fleshless form—

It reposes in ocean below.
And nevermore,
On the sea or shore,
Shall be heard the voice of Joe—poor Joe!
The ringing voice of Joe.

In the far, deep sea,
There lies he.
Yet he shall rise from his watery sleep,
And shake away his slumber deep—
When the angel's trumpet tones are heard
And earth and sea alike are stirred,
When the ghosts from above, and below,
Hurry along
In a sheeted throng—
We shall see once more our Joe—poor Joe!
The fleshless form of Joe.

Sonnet: The Sea

BY WILLIAM ALEXANDER

God of the Sea! How splendid is the scene
Displayed within thy palace bright and fair—
Where mermaids, pearl-decked, comb their flowing hair,
Or sport in garments of the gayest green!
About thy throne magnificent are piled
Vast crystal walls—bold, beautiful, and high—
While coral pillars in rich colors vie
With sea-flowers blooming in thy gardens wild.
Far other scenes and sights now do we view
As in thy depths we further downward wend:
Lo! There poor mortals' bones tighter blend;
There wrecks of vessels, with their darling crew.
Slumber they shall in death-sleep profound,
Till sea yield up his dead and the last trumpet sound.

The Dying Sailor To His Shipmates

BY *JAMES T. FIELDS*

Oh, wrap me in my country's flag,
And lay me in the cold, blue sea,
And let the roaring of the winds
My solemn requiem be;
And I shall sleep a pleasant sleep,
While storms above their vigils keep.

My captain brave shall read for me
The service of the silent dead,
And ye shall lower me in the waves,
When all the prayers are said;
And I will find my long, long home
Among the billows and the foam.

Farewell! My friends! Full many a league
We've sailed together on the deep;
Come! let's shake hands, I sail no more—
But, Shipmates! wherefore weep?
I'm bound above, my course is run.
I near the port; my voyage's done.

To A Sea Gull

BY ISAAC MCLELLAN, JR.

On thy swift and snow white wing,
Sea bird! whither dost thou tend?
Wheeling now in airy ring,
Loftier than the sailing cloud,
Poising now thy balanced plumes
Motionless in upper air,
Swooping now thy seaward flight
O'er the fretting yeast of waves,
Till the bursting billow's crest
Thy sharp-pointed pinion laves,
Battling on thy downy breast.
Now thou foldest up those wings,
Floating on the restless main,
Rising on the swelling billow,
Sinking in its gulf again,
Watching ever with keen eye
Where the shining fishes glide,

Then with talons and with beak,
Bearing them from ocean's tide.

Sea bird! Wildly calling sea-bird,
Whither on thy darling wing?
Hast thou the deep thunder heard,
Hast thou the red lightning seen?
See—the shadows of the cloud
Deepen o'er the evening sky;
See—the foam that crowns the surge
In a shadowy spray flies by!
Soon the darkness of the night
With the howling storm will come;
Hasten then thy devious flight
To thy nest beyond the foam!
Roars the deep, and raves the gale,
Yet all heedless thou dost stay,
Spreading out thy feathery sail
And pursuing still thy prey.
O'er the elemental strife,
Soundeth thy discordant scream—
Like the battle's piercing fife,
Swelling o'er the clang of arms.

Perhaps o'er the raging brine,
Painted against the lurid sky
On the gray horizon's verge,
Some lone bark dost thou descry—
Thou dost catch her shattered mast,
Thou dost see her fluttering sail,
Thou dost mark her banner cast

To the madly driving gale;
On her sloping, crowded deck,
On her strained masts thou dost see
Her wild seamen. Though to me
That far vessel seems a speck,
Thou dost see some aged sire
Wring his clasped hands in despair;
Some sweet maiden pale with fear,
Kneeling low in fervent prayer;
Some fair child with locks of gold,
Drenched by the relentless wave—
And all who walk that fatal deck
Soon are destined for the grave!

She advances! O'er her stern
Thou dost poise thy pinions now,
Hovering o'er each bending mast—
Stooping to the plunging prow!
Soon her grating keel will crash
O'er the billow-hidden rock;
Soon a frightful feast be spread
For thy wild and hungry flock;
Soon thy whetted beaks be red
With the corpse on ocean tossed;
Soon thy talons be entwined
In the bright locks of the lost!
Lo! The fearful scene is o'er.
Lo! The sea hath gained its prey.
O'er the tempest's hollow roar,
O'er the dashing of the spray,
Comes the loud convulsive cry

Of the devouring mariner;
Shrill, more shrill it echoes by,
Then sinks, and sinks, and all is o'er.

Wanderer of the pathless sea,
Keen of eye and strong of wing,
O'er how many shores, tell me,
Have those iron pinions passed?
In some calm and bright lagoon
Of the verdant Florida,
Circled by its coral reef,
Thou hast perhaps urged thy way;
Or by palmy woods that fringe
Cuba's ever-flowing shore,
Lending still a greener tinge
To the waves that round her roar;
Or by Greenland's stormy coast,
Far amid the polar seas,
Thou hast 'round the ice-bergs tossed,
Screaming in the northern breeze.

Sonnet: Ocean

BY WILLIAM ALEXANDER

Where hath thy voice, old Ocean, not been heard?
O'er every spot thy wild waves once have swept,
And o'er high hilltops hast thou boldly crept,
Obedient only to the Omnific Word.
Sits stillness mid dark Afric's wastes, yet there
Of old wert thou. The effigies of thy
Amazing primal denizens now lie
Sculptured on every crag; thy fish appear
Imbedded in the rock, so gray, whence hewed
Are Egypt's pyramids. Immensity
In thy broad bosom too, is seen to be,
Where storms assume terrific attitude.
One only makes thee calm and quiet stand,
Who holds thy waters all in "hollow of his hand."

Ocean Music at Evening

BY MARY E. LEE

Praised be thy music, ever-chaunting main!
Once more a pilgrim in the ancient fane
Of Nature, even at her altar stone,
I roam this eve, not lonely, though alone;
For though the day's bright chariot rolls its wheels
Low 'neath the horizon, and the twilight star
Scarce shows her jeweled forehead from afar,
Fairest 'mid ether's hall—and though there steals
No whispered perfume from the soft-lipped gale
That ever loves to kiss the twilight pale—
Yet is my spirit filled with joy profound
As thy sweet cadence, in deep organ swell,
Rises, then falls again with mystic spell,
Stilling to holy calm the world's disturbing sound.

"The Fairy of the Foam"

BY A. CLEVELAND COX, ESQ.

Loose, loose the sail!
A gentle gale is blowing from the shore,
And sunset's glow its sheen doth throw
Owasco's water's o'er.
Away we glide—aye, far away—
The ripple tide's a boon;
We leave this beach at parting day,
To sail beneath the moon.

And off we sweep—the glassy deep
Is glittering 'neath our prore;
And eyes as gay as starlight's ray
Are glancing from the shore.
Those eyes shall be our cynosure,
And guide our little sail—
For brightly beams their sparkle pure,
And charms away the gale.

Oh swiftly then! We'll back again,
When gaily o'er the stream
The soft starlight is dancing bright,
And shines the pale moonbeam.
And what though 'round us twilight dark
Be gathering as we roam—
Mary smiles to bless our bark,
"The Fairy of the Foam!"

The Sea

[Thomas Campbell]

Old ocean was,
Infinity of ages ere we breathed
Existence; and he will be beautiful
When all the living world that sees him now
Shall roll unconscious dust around the sun.
Quelling from age to age the vital throb
In human hearts, death shall not subjugate
The pulse that swells in *his* stupendous breast,
Or interdict his minstrelsy to sound
In thundering concert with the 'quiring winds;
But long as man to parent Nature owns
Instinctive homage, and in times beyond
The power of thought to reach, bard after bard
Shall sing thy glory, beatific Sea!

By the Summer Sea

BY *A. M. DANA*

A deep blue sea, and bluer sky,
White sails where their edges meet—
The waves come rolling grandly in,
And almost kiss my feet;
Wrecks lie below their dancing snow,
And wrecks in my heart there be;
But I bury them all beyond recall,
As I sit by the summer sea.

The sea-birds, wheeling overhead,
Cast shadows on the land;
While stopping, musingly I trace
Old mottos in the sand.
Fierce waves will roar on this peaceful shore,
And trials are waiting for me;
But I will not dread the storms ahead,
As I sit by the summer sea.

Sources

Alden, L. S. (1874). Little Maud. *Godey's Lady's Book*. Vol. 88, May, p. 456.

Alexander, W. (1852). Sonnet: Ocean. *Godey's Lady's Book*. Vol. 44, February, p. 129.

Alexander, W. (1852). Sonnet: The Sea. *Godey's Lady's Book*. Vol. 45, August, p. 166.

Author unknown. (1833). Going to Sea. *Ladies' Magazine*. Sarah J. Hale (Ed.). Vol. 6, August, p. 354.

Brainard, J. G. C. (1833). The Deep. *Godey's Lady's Book*. Vol. 6, January, p. 46.

Calvert, G. R. (1857). Gone Down at Sea. *Godey's Lady's Book*. Vol. 55, December, p. 538.

Campbell, T. (1832). The Sea. *Godey's Lady's Book*. Vol. 5, January, p. 61. (Unattributed excerpt from "The View from St. Leonard's.").

Cornwall, B. (1841). The Stormy Petrel. *Godey's Lady's Book.* Vol. 23, September, p. 138.

Cox, A. C. (1841). "The Fairy of the Foam." *Godey's Lady's Book.* Vol. 22, April, p. 184.

D. (1852). Outward Bound. *Godey's Lady's Book.* Vol. 44, February, p. 155.

Dana, A. M. (1868). By the Summer Sea. *Godey's Lady's Book.* Vol. 77, September, p. 241.

English, T. D. (1850). The Dead at Sea. *Godey's Lady's Book.* Vol. 41, December, p. 324.

Everallin. (1832). The Seaman's Bride. *Ladies' Magazine.* Sarah J. Hale (Ed.). Vol. 5, February, p. 70.

Fields, J. T. (1837). The Dying Sailor to His Shipmates. *Godey's Lady's Book.* Vol. 14, March, p. 112.

Fritz. (1851). At Sea. *Godey's Lady's Book.* Vol. 43, August, p. 115.

Geibel, E. (1864). Look On The Sea! *Godey's Lady's Book.* Vol. 68, January, p. 38. G. W. Birdseye, translator.

Good Literature: A Weekly Review of American and Foreign Publications, Volume III. No. 90, September 30, 1882. New York. The Masks of Authors Living and Dead, page 433.

Harrington, E. D. (1841). The Storm at Sea. *Godey's Lady's Book*. Vol. 22, April, p. 160.

Hilton, B. (1847). The Sea Bird. *Godey's Lady's Book*. Vol. 35, October, p. 179.

Keeling, R. J. (1850). Song to the Sea-Wave. *Godey's Lady's Book*. Vol. 40, January, p. 57.

L., G. W. (1831). Sunrise. *Ladies' Magazine*. Sarah J. Hale (Ed.). Vol. 4, May, p. 208.

Lee, M. E. (1845). Ocean Music at Evening. *Godey's Lady's Book*. Vol. 30, May, p. 210.

McLellan, I. Jr. (1842). To a Sea Gull. *Godey's Lady's Book*. Vol. 25, July, p. 6.

Miller, T. D. C. (1876). The Light-House Keeper's Daughter. *Godey's Lady's Book*. Vol. 92, June, p. 555.

Moise, I. (1847). To My Wife. *Godey's Lady's Book*. Vol. 35, September, p. 124.

Montagu, L. M. (1840). Like Music Stealing O'er the Water. *Godey's Lady's Book*. Vol. 20, June, p. 278. Music arranged by Sidney Pearson. Words unattributed in Godey's. Originally published as The Sailor's Bride, *The Metropolitan Magazine*. 1833, Vol. 1, p. 162.

Mortimer, L. (1849). The Sailor's Adieu to His Wife. *Godey's Lady's Book*. Vol.39, November, p. 345.

O'Quill, M. (1848). The Waves and Their Dead. *Godey's Lady's Book*. Vol. 37, November, p. 254.

P., J. Q. (1839). I Love the Sea, the Mighty Sea. *Godey's Lady's Book*. Vol. 17, March, p. 114.

Rebecca. (1835). To the Sea. *The American Ladies' Magazine*. Sarah J. Hale (Ed.). Vol. 8, October, p. 560.

Shepard, E. D. G. (1854.) *Cut-flowers: A Collection of Poems*. J. G. Holland (Ed.)

Sigourney, L. H. (1829). To The Sea. *Ladies' Magazine*. Sarah J. Hale (Ed.). Vol. 2, February, p. 53.

Simms, W. G. (1842). Calm at Sea. *Godey's Lady's Book*. Vol. 24, June, p.335.

Simms, W. G. (1849). Apostrophe to the Sea. *Godey's Lady's Book*. Vol. 38, January, p. 41.

Wells, A. M. (1829). Hope. *Ladies' Magazine*. Sarah J. Hale (Ed.). Vol. 2, March, p. 103.

32695130R00051

Made in the USA
Charleston, SC
24 August 2014